Compliance Tales & Travels

Patrick Henz

DEDICATION

To travelers, even at home.

CONTENTS

FOREWORD

"Disruption" is in fashion today, to stop the current and give opportunity to the new. Disruption does not automatically mean that something new will be implemented, but that a break can be used to think about the status quo and potential alternatives. A new decision-making process will choose between continuing on the known path or switch to a new one.

A travel disrupts the daily-routine and sometimes even pushes the individual out of their personal comfort-zones. "Traveling educates" is not only a phrase, but new locations and meeting other people are always a source of inspiration. The individual connects the new impression with his or her actual life and tasks. After the time off, such new ideas can make the person re-think his or her tasks and, hopefully, make such more effective.

The French author Marcel Proust analyzed: *"The real voyage consists not in seeking new landscapes but in having new eyes."* In 2020, COVID-19 let to a different kind of journey, a slow journey in time without changing the location. An opportunity to use the time to edit some of my older texts to include them into two new Compliance books. Both "Compliance Travels" and "Business Tales from the Racetrack" have their own unique theme. Nevertheless, I liked th idea of reviving last century's concept of omnibus-movies. One film but telling three or four independent stories. A popular concept particularly in the 1960s. One example is "Spirits of the Dead", where Federico Fellini directed the third segment "Toby Dammit". The former Shakespeare actor Toby Dammit receives a role for a movie set in Rome, where besides his salary he receives a golden Ferrari as bonus. Slowly he loses his mind and races around a surreal city. Fellini was aware of Ferrari's ability to offer customized cars for special clients, as they did for example for Roberto Rosselini or Gianni Agnelli. For the movie he used a Ferrari 330 LMB, commissioned by Fiorenzo Fantuzzi to create a unique coach for the chassis. The result became known as "the golden Ferrari", surreal as the film itself, as after the filming, the chassis was reunited with its original body, while the golden spyder body became re-used to fit on a Ferrari 330 2+2, only to get lost in time.

With these ideas, welcome to the book!

Patrick Henz, Atlanta 2020

Compliance Travels

1 THE LEONARDO COMPLIANCE FORMULA

By car, the small city of Vinci is around 41 kilometers away from Florence. Today around 14,300 citizens live here. More than 500 years ago, Leonardo was born near this place and based on the tradition, received his name "Leonardo di ser Piero da Vinci". As universal genius, talented artist and curious in all aspects, he became the ideal of the Renaissance time.

In his famous "Vitruvian Man" he realistically pictured a man from different angles. Leonardo not only understood the outside, but also human psychology, as his quote *"It is easier to resist at the beginning than at the end."* confirms. The beginning of a potential Compliance deviation is the best time to contact your Ethics & Compliance Officer. The employee considers this, while the decision depends on the perceived benefits and costs for doing so.

As Leonardo was a man of science, we can convert his idea into a formula, starting with some basic definitions:

r) Estimated Compliance risk: The estimated negative impact for the company and society. (Empathy and involvement in society leads to a higher estimated Compliance risk.)

b) Anticipated benefit of Compliance: The estimated positive impact of the Compliance Officer solving the problem.

c) Cost of Information: The estimated cost to contact the Compliance Officer and / or to involve him / her. This also includes an estimated negative or positive impact for the employee, for example potential disciplinary action or an expected whistleblower-award. For the last case, the cost would turn into benefit.

The defined variables we can include into the "**Leonardo Compliance Formula**", where we distinguish between two cases:

$$(1/r) > b - c$$

When getting aware of a potential Compliance risk, the employee estimates what impact this could cause for the company, society and him- or herself. If the individual received an adequate Compliance training, this guess gets qualified. Nevertheless, he / she is no expert on the topic, so the estimation could be right, but also wrong. For the company, the best solution would be that the employee would contact his / her Compliance Officer. If the individual would do this, depends on how the employee anticipates the benefit, and how cost-intensive relevant Compliance information and decisions are. If 1/"estimated risk" is assumed to be higher than the anticipated benefit minus the costs to receive this information, the employee will not seek to contact Compliance. As the risk estimation can be wrong, this can lead to a Compliance problem, a relevant risk for the company.

In the second scenario we have the opposite case: $(1/r) < b - c$

If benefit minus costs is higher than 1/"estimated risk"; the Compliance department will be involved. In this scenario, the preferences of the employee and the employer are aligned. To reach this status, companies can work with the three variables:

- Foster employees' Compliance knowledge, so that they are able to judge correctly potential risks. For example, with adequate training (basic training for all, plus tailor-made workshops depending on the different job-profiles).

- Establish the Compliance Officer as a trusted advisor and enabler, which can offer relevant information and act efficiently. This maximizes the anticipated benefit of Compliance involvement.

- Lower the cost of information. Compliance must be close to the business and easy to reach. Additionally, an award for positive behavior up to for whistleblowers can be implemented. If possible, tools like smart phones and apps can ensure communication availability 24 hours and 7 days a week. The last can be reached with an internal Compliance Wiki plus a connected chat-bot to answer frequently asked questions and support finding the adequate answers inside the Wiki.

- Connect Compliance with company and personal values. Based on Leon Festinger's "theory of cognitive dissonance", a potential wrong-doing leads to pressure inside the employee, as (potential) actions would not be compatible with own attitudes and values.[1] Lowering psychological pressures would be another benefit of Compliance involvement.

- Connect Compliance with the company's sustainability strategy, to foster that employees understand the interaction between corruption and macro-economics.

---

[1] Festinger, Leon (1957): "A Theory of Cognitive Dissonance"

Just as Leonardo predicts, the longer you are walking down the wrong path, the more difficult it gets to resist the future wrongdoing, as with advancing time also the cost of information rise. This includes that the employee must admit his / her personal failure (similar to "losing face" in various cultures) and must assume in parallel that the correct behavior (report the wrongdoing and return to the correct path) will be paired with a disciplinary sanction.

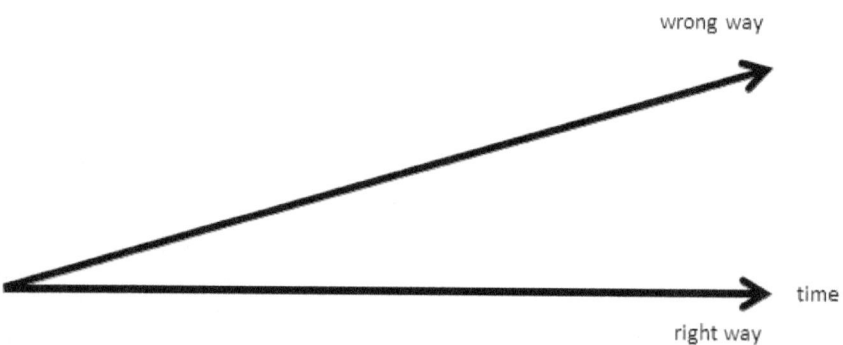

Perception is important. The employee must understand that he / she is on the wrong path. In many cases this is not the case right from the beginning. The employee perceives him or herself as on the right track, but then more or less suddenly understands that this is not the case. Hereby the perception can be everywhere in-between the absolute black and white. Through the employee's eyes he / she can be on any imagine imaginable path on or above the right one, even above the wrong way.

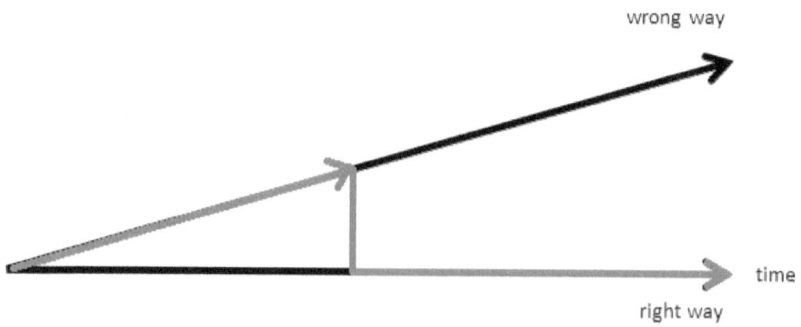

Again, Compliance workshops support employees not just to stay on the right path, but also if they leave this path, to recognize this as early as possible. To reach this goal, a workshop cannot limit itself on pure teaching of information but must include real-life case discussions and psychological stress scenarios, responsible for the ethical blindness-phenomenon.[2]

According to Leonardo, it is easier to resist a future wrong-doing (=continuing to walk down the wrong path), if you are still in the beginning, at or soon after a decision. This is because the longer you are on the wrong track, the bigger gets the gap, and the more difficult it is to jump from the wrong to the right path. Meaning, if you want to return to the right way, you must communicate with your Compliance Officer and a) commit your wrong-doing to yourself and b) to the company. Most organizations have a range of disciplinary sanctions, which starts from nothing, if it is plausible that the deviation was a pure accident, up to separation of the employee from the company, if it is a severe case. The cost of information gets higher with the time. Implementing a whistle-bower award may lead to negative costs, especially if the deviation was caused by various employees. In this scenario the whistleblower would be understood as informant (similar to cartel cases).

Based on Leonardo, we extend the formula and include "g = gap" into our calculation:

$$(1/r) < b - c - g$$

Herby, the gap includes:

v) Own responsibility for wrong-doing.

s) Severity of the wrong decision (the angular degree between both paths).

t) Time.

---

[2] Palazzo, Guido / Krings, Franciska / Hoffrage, Ulrich (2012): "Ethical Blindness"

$$(1/r) < b - c - (v * s * t)$$

According to mathematics, if any of these values (v,s,t) would become 0, g becomes 0:

v=0 : The employee perceives no responsibility for the deviation, "it was an accident".

s=0 : The employee does not perceive a negative impact on the culture and values of the company or other stakeholders. A relevant Compliance risk may not be perceived as severe if the employee perceives law and ethics as drifted apart.

t=0 : The employee is still in the process of decision making.

If 1/"anticipated compliance risk" is lower than the benefit of possible compliance involvement, minus the costs of information and the gap, the employee most-likely will continue on the wrong path without making the situation transparent, as it is easier to give in the temptation to follow the wrong path than to resist it and return to right one.

The Compliance Officer can work on these topics:

- Responsibility: Workshops can discuss the responsibility of employees, especially regarding approvals and signatures. Responsibility is not limited to the company but also includes the society.
- Severity: A good Compliance training is not limited to laws and regulations, but explains what is behind, like cost of corruption (for the company and society). Based on personal values, employees may perceive a higher personal guilt than the Compliance risks exposed to the company.

As the flow of time is still no changeable value, it should be as easy as possible to contact the Compliance Officer, including communication channels, distance and attitude.

This formula is not meant to be a mathematical equation, but should explain the relation, in which the single factors stand with each other. With this understanding, the formula works as inspiration to update the existing Compliance system.

Patrick Henz

2 THE OWL PRINCIPLE

Many Ethics & Compliance-departments and -companies use the compass as their logo. What about another approach, maybe the owl would be an appropriate representation?

In many cultures the owl is an admired symbol for knowledge and wisdom, even if at the same time it is also a hunter, a predator.

Based on the job-description, a Compliance Officer must be an expert in Compliance. A list of needed sub-skills and knowledge easily can fill two pages. Nevertheless, this is only the beginning of the journey. The Compliance Officer wants to reach the next level and become a trusted expert for its colleagues. To reach this goal, it is not enough to limit on Compliance or approach legal & ethics topics, but mandatory to get at least a basic understanding of the complete business. With the required knowledge, the Compliance Officer can climb the step to become a trusted advisor. This includes the perception that the Compliance Officer is not only qualified but also has the adequate ability to support its colleagues.

The "Pygmalion Effect" can support a positive corporate culture. If the Compliance Officer (employee A) treats its colleague (employee B) with respect, this confirms B's positive self-esteem and is a respectful person. By imposing this value, in return B treats A respectfully. A now perceives B's respectful behavior and concludes that B is a respectful person. A cycle is created. Respect opens the opportunity for Compliance to enter employee B's circle of trust.

If the Compliance Officer is perceived as knowledgeable and respectful, B will open to A, ask if needed and in return consider its pieces of advice.[3]

Visibility is needed, so that employees can perceive their Compliance Officer as a trusted colleague, who is not just talking about Compliance, but living it as a good example. It is helpful not to perceive everybody as a

---

[3] Henz, Patrick (2019): "Tomorrow's Business Ethics – Philip K. Dick vs. W. Edwards Deming"

potential risk factor but to start with the idea that more than 99% of the employees are good and honest people, making their best effort daily for the benefit of the company. These people are to be protected and prepared so that they will not get into trouble via accident (or through a case caused by the less than 1% outcast, which you may have). Such behavior requires self-discipline and -motivation but supports the Compliance Officer to establish itself as trusted advisor, aligned with the owl's wisdom. What is missing now is also to address the predator-side.

The success of the Compliance system primally not depends on the sophisticated processes and controls, but the perceived tone-from-the-top. Employees want to see their management (top to direct manager) complying with the system. To be credible, this includes also how management, including Compliance Officer, handles potential deviations up to violations to anti-corruption laws. Employees understand the positive message of a Compliance system and expect that deviations lead to predictable consequences. The Compliance Officer must ensure this. Fairness is a relevant value. A Compliance system must be as strong as possible, but not more to avoid non-necessary bureaucracy. The last would be perceived by the employees as disturbing unfair burden to their daily tasks.

Accordingly, the Compliance Officer must act as enabler, thanks to a risk assessment understanding the requirements and if indicated, discussing with management to change non-efficient processes and controls. That way, employees perceive Compliance as enforcer of processes, but also enabler to update such guidelines; Compliance achieves the status of a trusted enabler, aligned with the owl's nature being a predator. Combing both paths, wisdom and predator leads to appreciation and respect.

The renaissance artist Giambologna (1529 – 1608) was originally born in Flanders, but already in young years went to Rome for studying classical sculpture. One of his most famous works is the Apennine Colossus statue in the Pratolino Medici Park. Less known, the same artist also created a life-size owl statue for the same park. Before Giambologna, Niccolò Machiavelli (1469-1527) worked as advisor for the Medici family. And indeed, the Owl Principle aligns with one of Machiavelli's famous quotes: *"Hence it comes that all armed prophets have been victorious, and all unarmed prophets have been destroyed."*[4] (Later reduced to the simple: *"Before else, be armed"*).

If the company wants to ensure that values and guidelines get followed, it must ensure that violations to them not only get identified but also remediated. Nobody in the company stands over its code of conduct (on which guidelines, policies and tools are set up on). Remediation must be adequate for the deviation, there can be no different answers for different levels of employees. If the deviation indicates it, the company must take the hard decision to separate the employee from the company, even if this means a loss of important knowledge and complying with the difficult local labor laws. This is the only way that you can earn the respect of the

---

[4] Machiavelli, Niccolò (ca'. 1543): "The Prince"

employees. In a company, tone from the top, implemented tools and guidelines can only be a starting point for each employee, as everyone must decide for him or herself, if the company requirements can be accepted or not. If not, the employee should pro-actively take the step to leave the organization. If the individual cannot or do not want to take this step, there is a risk that eventually, he or she will commit violations to company values and guidelines. As each person is different, including different personal values and attitudes, it is impossible to eliminate the risk of having such a person inside the company. It is in the best interest of the company to identify them, this to protect itself, but also all other employees.

Armed is not limited to physical force but applies also to arguments. Machiavelli aligns with the Owl Principle, especially the parts "trusted expert" and "trusted enabler."

He wrote further: *"…when they depend upon their own resources and can employ force, they seldom fail."*[5] An ethics, compliance or internal audit department must be independent, adequately stuffed and financed to ensure the efficient combination wisdom and predator.

Besides with Machiavelli's The Prince, the Owl Principle also aligns with newer concepts, such as "The Trust Triangle" by Frances Frei and Anne Morriss. Here both authors define trust with the tree edges "logic", "authenticity" and "empathy".[6] Logic relates to the predator-side, the Compliance Officer is a trusted enabler and will solve the identified problem or answer my questions. Authenticity and empathy relate to the wisdom-side. The employee perceives the Compliance Officer as a real human, who is understanding and caring for other humans.

Robotics is another topic, which can be traced back to the Italian Renaissance, as it was one of the topics the universal genius Leonardo da Vinci worked on. In its Codex Atlanticus he described a self-propelled card.[7] A small vehicle powered (1480) by two symmetric springs. This

---

[5] Machiavelli, Niccolò (ca'. 1543): "The Prince"

[6] Frei, Frances X. / Morriss, Anne (2020): "Begin with Trust"

[7] Da Vinci, Leonardo (ca. 1478 – 1519): "Codex Atlanticus"

featured a reprogrammable steering and could had been used for example on the stage of a theatre. Later in 1495 he presented an even more sophisticated machine, the first robot. Like today's retro-fits, Leonardo equipped a medieval armor with a mechanism to enable the mechanical knight to stand, sit, rise its visor and even independently maneuver its arms.

Today's technical developments like Robotic Process Automation liberate the Ethics & Compliance Officer from routine works as exporting data and create samples & reports, while Artificial Intelligence is superior in the identification of suspicious patterns in payments. As consequence, the Compliance Officer can use the opportunity to have more face-time with employees and other stakeholders. A limited number of expert-skills perceive devaluation, but general skills like empathy, creativity and ingenuity become more important. A return of the renaissance human, combining arts with science.

Important, one aspect of the Owl-Principle differs from Machiavelli. Once asked if it is better to be loved or feared, he answered that both are important, but difficult to combine. If in doubt, feared is more important.[8] The owl goes less to extremes, as it aims to combine wisdom with respect. Both concepts are compatible, but the ideal equilibrium should be more towards wisdom, as the focus of an efficient Compliance program should be on prevention.

---

[8] Machiavelli, Niccolò (ca. 1543): "The Prince"

3 TRAVELOGUE: VISIT OF TO THE MONASTERY BINARIO

A visit to the Monastery Binario, located in the Tuscany region, shows the amazing benefits of intelligent systems and artificial intelligence.

1609 was an important year for Galileo Galilei, first he perfected the telescope, then he used his invention to study the Earth's satellite, gaining important knowledge of the surface of the moon. For him, religion and science were not contradictory, but rather two sides of the same coin.

After leaving the city center of Florence via the Ponte Vecchio to slowly climb the hills, I now stood in front of the observatory which was used by Galileo in 1609/10. It was halfway to the famous Giardino Bardini. Located outside the center, it was ideal for exploring the night sky. The building itself was closed, but there was a small shelf before the entrance offering various flyers. One got my attention. An inconspicuous page printed with Galileo's famous saying: *"Mathematics is the alphabet that God used to describe the universe."* It read below: *"Logic is divine, everyone is free in their pursuit of knowledge. Experience the Monastery of San Binario."* The printed address indicated a location about an hour away from Florence.

I had not planned anything special for the next day, so I took my rental car and headed there. On winding roads, I arrived at lonely monastery. It was not a typical tourist magnet, and I seemed to be the only visitor. After I parked my car at the empty parking lot, I went to the main entrance and knocked on the gate. A monk, who later introduced himself as Brother Alan, opened and granted me admission: *"Welcome to the Monastery of San Binario."* I entered and was amazed by the interior of the building. A fitting mix of Renaissance and 1960s futurism. *"Surprised?"*, Brother Alan asked me. *"A little,"* I replied. He explained that God manifests through clear logic. Nothing is more sublime than mathematics, pure truth without weak human interpretations and descriptions. The brotherhood has made it its mission to honor God by respecting all members' individual existence and acquiring knowledge based on their talents and preferences. All of them are connected by the fact that they are experts in the field of artificial intelligence. Together they created an algorithm that analyzes the monks' abilities to derive a business model for the abbey.

Brother Alan led me through the building to leave it on the opposite side. His goal was to see the nearby cowsheds. Ten years ago, the well-known Chianina cattle were bred here. After the monks had accumulated additional knowledge at the various universities, the AI recommended switching to beer brewery. After this was successful and the monks continued to learn, the AI advised to reduce the beer and to focus on business consulting. Since then, they have used their conference rooms to teach how Industry 4.0 works effectively together with self-organizing teams. This philosophy was important to the monks, the AI did not dictate how they should act, nor did other organizational functions. The individual had all the freedom to realize himself according to his own ideas and thus to find fulfillment. This happened with ongoing learning, to honor God, which, regarding the self-organizing monastic structures, did not require a head besides the Lord.

It was getting late, so I said goodbye to Brother Alan and wanted to return to my Airbnb. When I got to the car, I saw the surprise. The stone path to the monastery had led to a flat tire. Brother Alan saw the dilemma from the gate and waved me to come. He offered me a room that was normally reserved for the participants at the conferences. Since there were no events that day, the rooms were all free. I received the room "010". To my surprise, it was not monastery sparse but offered all the amenities of a modern hotel. The mattress was hard but comfortable, so I got a good night's sleep.

Since there were currently no other visitors to the monastery, the kitchen was not occupied. The next morning, when I left my room and went to the breakfast room, a brother greeted me with panini and coffee. He gave me company and introduced himself as Brother Konrad. I noticed a leather bracelet with a technical gadget on his right joint. It did not have a screen, just a row of LEDs, one of which glowed green. The monk had already finished breakfast and was drinking a cappuccino. With the first sip I saw that the green LED on his bracelet went out. He laughed when he noticed that this surprised me. *"A minor sin. This is a Dante unit,"* he explained the bracelet to me. *"Dante unit?"*, I asked. Before I could formulate my question, he started: *"Yes, Dante, named after the poet and philosopher. Author of the Divida Commedia, where he describes his journey from hell to paradise."* The Dante unit was practically a collection of sensors that the monks connected to an AI to analyze their daily activities, whether they were a benefit or harm for society. If the AI came to a positive verdict, the number of green glowing LEDs increased; if the judgment were negative, the number decreased, or could even become negative, in this case glowing red LEDs. The redder lamps, the longer one would have to burn in hellfire after death before going to heaven. Red could be reduced by doing good deeds, including prayers. *"Import is the quality of the deeds, not the pure quantity,"* continued Brother Konrad. *"The Dante unit has various sensors, including skin resistance measurement and a microphone. The underlying AI can evaluate this data to see whether I meant the words honestly or just simply recited them."* But the bracelet was not just passive. If the AI considered it necessary that the individual monk or the whole of Binario Monastery should execute positive deeds, it could communicate this via a beep tone. Important for the brotherhood, the unit was limited to the information of necessity per se but gave no clue how the deeds should look like. The AI should not unnecessarily affect the relationship between humans and creator.

Brother Konrad pointed to the window overlooking the parking lot. I saw two monks about to change the tire on my rental car. *"One more green LED for the two"*, the monk laughed.

4 THE NECCESARY EVIL

Staying at home, as in the times of COVID-19, gives the opportunity to spend more time on the various streaming platforms. Important to follow the advice of experienced travelers and leave the beaten paths. Especially Netflix, which includes many local productions from all over the world, which turn out to be real treasures. One example is the Italian-British series "Medici: Masters of Florence". Of course, not all fiction are facts, nevertheless a precious inspiration to have a look into the Renaissance (15th to 16th century). A time when in the Western hemisphere, humanity left the darkness of the middle-age and rediscovered the importance & beauty of art & science. Holistically understood by Leonardo da Vinci: *"To develop a complete mind: Study the science of art; Study the art of science. Learn how to see. Realize that everything connects to everything else."* This philosophy translated into education leads to STREAM (Science, Technology, Reading, Engineering, Arts, Mathematics) or STEAM (Science, Technology, Engineering, Arts, Mathematics).

Already in the very first episode of the series, Giovanni de' Medici (1360 – 1429) says: *"It is sometimes necessary to do some bad in order to achieve a greater good."* Later this quote gets repeated by his elder son Cosimo (1389 – 1464). There is no historical evidence that they really spoke these words. The question is, could they have said it?

Niccolò Machiavelli (1469 – 1527), advisor to the Medici family described in chapter VIII of his famous book "The Prince" the need of a prince to rule with cruelty.[9] Definitely, cruelty is "bad", but could be used, if it serves the higher good, like fostering the ruler's position, which he presumed as "good", as the prince is the best choice to ensure a prospering region. To translate it into mathematics, if we have an evil-action with the value of "-1" and a positive results of "+3" (fostering own position), together with sole alternative option of evil=0, but a less favorable outcome of "+1" (a less competent ruler will replace me), we get:

$$(-1) + 3 > 0 +1$$
$$= \qquad 2 > 1$$

Conclusion: Machiavelli understands the evil as necessary and recommends the action. Utilitarianism raises the question of values. The Stanford Encyclopedia of Philosophy defines: *"Though there are many varieties of the view discussed, utilitarianism is generally held to be the view that the morally right action is the action that produces the most good."*[10] A clear mathematical reason, nevertheless a sophisticated philosophical discussion what produces the most good, based on culture, a pure counting of individuals does not solve the problem. Societies user their cultural beliefs as a base to create a constitution and laws. If the evil was not committed in a not-yet-defined grey zone, it is now sanctionable. If law gets adequately executed, after an evil should not follow a positive result for the one who committed such.

Many of today's regions are ruled by impunity, what returns the possibility of the necessary evil. Compliance Officer may face such discussions, as business colleagues may argue (falsely) that corruption would be a part of the culture or that without bribery it would not be possible to conduct business. On the other hand, they may rationalize to rise the positive outcome of the planned actions, not only for them personally, but for the whole organization. For example:

- Action: Everybody is doing it.
- Action: Corruption is normal.

---

[9] Machiavelli, Niccolò (ca. 1543): "The Prince"

[10] Stanford Encyclopedia of Philosophy (2014): "The History of Utilitarianism"

- Result: Winning the project is not only important for me, but for the company's overall strategy.
- Result: The competitors have less competitive solutions; it would be in the client's best interest if they chose our solution.

It is up to management and the Compliance Officer to counter such arguments. Even if employees should be convinced also on ethical level, globally valid anti-corruption laws such as the US Foreign Corrupt Practices Act (FCPA) or the UK Bribery Act make it clear that evil is forbidden everywhere in the world.

As the inclined leader observed, Niccolò Machiavelli lived around a decade later than Giovanni de' Medici. Nevertheless, the concept of the necessary evil was known in the antique and even the Bible. Machiavelli grew up in Florence. As the city was deeply related to Medici, it can be assumed that the famous family consciously and subconsciously influenced him.

5 BALSAMIC VINEGAR

The city of Modena is not only famous for sports-cars like Ferrari, Lamborghini and Maserati, but also for its delicious food, including being home of the traditional (and certified) balsamic vinegar. Accordingly, visitors should plan to not only visit the company museums, but also to spend a day in the medieval down-town and enjoy the offered high-quality local meals.

Authentic balsamic vinegar is made from a reduction of cooked grape must, with no other ingredients.[11] Furthermore, this grape must be aged for five years in wooden barrels to produce the famous sweet and vicious taste.[12] Higher quality balsamic vinegars even have to age for twelve (affinato) or 25 (extra vecchio) years. Besides this, there is a geographic limitation for farmers to produce this coveted product.

---

[11] The Balsamic Guy (fetched 2020): "Balsamic Types"

[12] May, Sheila (2015): "Classification of Balsamic Vinegar"

The strict requirements lead to an upscale price and opens a potential market for cheaper products. Producers reduce the aging time and add additional ingredients to create a similar taste. To market the product, the producers are interested that potential clients perceive it as near as possible to the high-price certified vinegar. This can be reached by using similar labeling and wording, and sometimes even faking the original certificates.

Internal tests and external certification are relevant procedures to ensure transparency and quality. On the other hand, strong competition puts pressure on companies and its employees, as it may be challenging to combine quality with low costs. Pressure rises if the sales department already sold the product before engineering had the opportunity to review the possibility of delivering on the promise. Tasks should be challenging, but possible. The last could be perceived as missing respect from the employer towards the employee. As consequence, employees lose their respect for the company and try to bypass internal controls and processes, especially if bonus payments depend on solving the problem.

So far, Engineering and Production are no classic target-groups for advanced Ethics & Compliance workshops. Nevertheless, a modern approach must be to protect good employees, if needed against themselves, as the joined pressure of various biases may lead to the "Ethical Blindness"-phenomena.[13] The best prevention is to make employees aware of the vulnerabilities. With discussion of real-life examples (and in the last years there had been various cases to learn from), employees can understand potential dilemmas and how to adequately act in such scenarios. Of course, learning is only one side of the medal. The same importance must establish adequate processes to support the employees. Depending the individual company, Engineering and Production could be involved already in the creation of an offer. Furthermore, employees should be empowered to protest if tasks get perceived as impossible, if needed to enable them to anonymously report such cases.

---

[13] Palazzo, Guido / Krings, Franciska / Hoffrage, Ulrich (2012): "Ethical Blindness"

6 *"X NEVER, EVER MARKS THE SPOT."*

The third Indiana Jones movie brought the famous professor and adventurer to Venice.[14] Before the sudden travel he still explained in his archeology lecture: *"We do not follow maps to buried treasure, and X never, ever marks the spot."* This only to prove himself wrong, as the floor of antique library (shown as the San Barnaba-church), marked the entrance to the city's catacombs with a big X.

X never marks the spot, similar is also valid for an efficient Compliance system. As every company is different, so are the underlying risks and opportunities. The times of unlimited budgets are long gone. It is the Compliance Officer's task to identify together with management and other key employees' potential risks and opportunities. Aligned with the risk appetite of the company, adequate measures must be implemented to avoid, reduce, shift or accept the risks.

---

[14] Spielberg, Steven (1989): "Indiana Jones and the Last Crusade"

When thinking about potential actions, one relevant question could be what the company founder would do. This is not only in the general risk discussion, but also inside training and workshops. If the organization still is the position that the founder is active, Compliance can elaborate Compliance statements from him or her. If this is not the case anymore, the corporate archive could be a place to go.

The Vatican's secret archive (official name: "Vatican Apostolic Archive"), is less mysterious as movies often present it. Most part of information can be accessed by the qualified public, like for example, authors, scholars, historians and other scientists. These documents provide fascinating insights from the world's oldest still active organization. To support the interest from all over the world, documents are accessible via the archive's website. This also includes the files from the trail where Galileo Galilei recanted his concept of heliocentrism.

The archives of many companies include information about inventions, products and factories. But also, often the founder's biographies, including career and personal life. Such information can align a Compliance system with the original ideas and values. For most entrepreneurs, their own company was more than just source of income. They planned for the long-term, as they wanted to change the market or even the world. To reach this, sustainability was necessary. In addition, they saw the company not only for themselves, but also for the generations to come. Compliance is part of the company's sustainability approach. Based on legal, ethics and business philosophy, it wants to ensure that the organization can conduct business today, and tomorrow and the day after tomorrow.

Business Tales from the Racetrack

7 FROM AUTO RACING TO BEHAVIORAL SCIENCE

"What has instructed all of the world's builders of safe, efficient cars? Auto racing. Any theory, any laboratory experiment needs practical support, and only the race can offer it because during the race the driver submits the car and its parts to intense, unpredictable, unthinkable testing." As Enzo Ferrari explained , he had the machine in mind, but auto racing is also the ultimate test for human behavior. This, as not only the drivers act at the limit, but the whole crew, what includes, for example, the mechanics and commando stand.

All involved individuals are full of adrenaline and have only extremely limited time to make the required decisions, a dangerous combination. The stress of the race-day pushes them out of their comfort zones. This as adrenaline is a neurotransmitter to alert all cells that the individual is an extraordinary situation, which requires the maximal use of all muscles and senses.

Each race is different, and each second something unpredictable can happen, to which driver and team must react to. US-psychologist Walter Bradford Cannon concluded 1915 in his theory of *"fight or flight"* that a high level of adrenaline can block the individual's ability for logical thinking, this as the hormone increases the heart rate to enlarge blood pressure, expand the air passages of the lungs, enlarge the pupil, redistribute blood to the muscles and alter the body's metabolism, as to maximize blood glucose levels.[15] Thanks to evolution, adrenaline acts as a motivator. Produced in low levels, it triggers to start of cognitive processes. In high levels it provokes that the individual perceives to be in a survival situation and the primary task is to get out of this as soon as possible.[16] Originally required to escape from angry mammoths or other dangerous animals, today's drivers need this condition to push their-selves to the limited.

---

[15] Ivan Becrzi: Walter Cannon's "Fight or Flight Response" - "Acute Stress Response"

German business coach Tom Senninger developed in 2000 the Learning Zone Model, where the individual is most of the time in its personal Comfort Zone. For personal growth it is required to leave this state and enter the Learning Zone to seek new experiences. The individual could motivate itself for this, or react to external stimuli. If the self- or external-motivation gets too high, the effect becomes contra-productive, as the individual reaches the Panic Zone. The different zones correlate with the regarding levels of adrenaline (Comfort > Learning > Panic).

In business, management may use pictures as "race", "competition" or even "war" to motivate their employees, especially if they are sales-related. Based on this description, employees produce higher levels of adrenaline, which may interfere with their capacity for logical thinking. Even if they have strong personal values, high level of stress may lead to inadequate decision-making processes, where the latter behavior is incompatible with the individuals' values.

Single decisions may get perceived as fundamental, as victories in single races or ensuring a "must win"-project. Especially when a sudden opportunity to overtake an opponent gets perceived, the race drivers try to take it, sometimes without an adequate decision-making process. The results could be a race-accident where both cars must retire from the race, or even an unfair maneuver where one car drives into the other and pushes it out of the race. Other possibilities are the usage of illegal short-cuts. With this, winning a single race may jeopardize the overall goal to ensure the championship.

Driving behind a competitor and slowly closing the gap normally does not lead to driving errors, as the driver has a plan and is able to study the competitor from safe distance (Learning Zone). But closing a gap and overtaking are two different chapters. The opponent is aware of the risk and tries to block the following driver. Such behavior is difficult to predict, so that the following driver cannot elaborate a plan for safe passing. Overtaking means more points, more money and, important, more acknowledgement. The direct fight in combination with speed and time-limit causes a stress moment (Panic Zone). But even if the race is still long and a more passive driving-style would present a better opportunity for success, often the race driver tries to use the first perceived opportunity to pass the competitor. Already here the high stress level blocks the ability for logical decision-making processes, so that perceived opportunities are often not real existent. This leads to accidents in extreme situations, to accidents between two team-colleagues or eliminations directly at the start. This as humans tend to focus on the now, instead of the long-term goal.

Such situations allow us a precious insight into human nature and how individuals act on the limit. A situation which could not be created in an experiment or laboratory, as ethics forbids us to push individuals up to the limits of their panic zones.

As the risk is identified and also the possible risk-groups, the question is, what can be done to mitigate it? Behavior is partly based on information, so one strategy to reduce stress is to reduce the level of the unknown. A case-discussion or a role-play about pros and contras of potential behavior should lead to the result that the driver will develop a (hopefully) positive attitude to not provoke accidents, or in short to *"think before drive"*. Companies can conduct workshops, where employees get confronted with different potential scenarios, where they must decide. The results get discussed to analyze their impact on company, the individual itself and other stakeholders, including society. Knowing the potential impact raises the employee's empathy for all affected sides and triggers even in stressful situations to elaborate an adequate decision-making process and not let yourself *"rushed into a decision"*.

This theory gets confirmed by Oliver Sheldon's and Ayelet Fishbach's study for the Rutgers Business School: *"If people want to avoid unethical behavior, it may help to anticipate situations where they will be tempted and consider how acting upon such temptations fits with their long-term goals or beliefs about their own morality."*[17] As conclusion, an Ethics & Compliance training can work as an *"ethical vaccination"*, as the positive attitude will not be activated now, but stays as *"antibodies"* inside the person and help to make it immune to the regarding temptations. To ensure an effective protection, such vaccinations must be

---

[17] Sheldon, Oliver J. / Fishbarch, Ayelet (2017): "Unethical Temptation"

repeated from time to time. This is especially relevant for situations where decisions must be made inside seconds. The individual detects the risky situation and thanks to the earlier workshops already has an adequate attitude (which could be understood as a *"script"*), no extended decisions making process is required.

For the case that all these moral arguments do not work, the drivers must be aware that there are efficient controls implemented. There are cameras around the track to detect all aspects of the race and race stewards speak out penalties for illegal behavior, no one is above the regulations.

To make it as easy as possible for an employee to detect a potential risk situation, workshops must be as specific as possible, including, for example, information about the project and region. Especially if the employees travel there a first time and do not know local culture and language. Often situations in foreign countries get falsely perceived and due to this, lead to wrong behavior. This includes under- or over-estimating risks.

Based on this understand, race weekends traditionally include a track-walk and driver-briefing to analyze the particular risks of a race-track and specific rules. Today such risk assessments get supported by Industry 4.0 with its possibility to identify potential patterns and predict future scenarios. Furthermore, thanks to internet, laptops and smart-phones, individuals can stay continuously connected with the Cloud, but also directly with their colleagues at the company. In Formula One, the drivers and cars are connected with the team's command stands, including their computers. A modern F1 car can have between 150 & 300 sensors and send this information to the team. This data fosters the drivers' and teams' knowledge and decisions.

A discussion or a role-play (Formula One drivers often use video-games) about such pros and cons should lead to the result that the driver will develop a (hopefully) positive attitude to not provoke accidents, if one day he would be in a similar scenario. For this, an Ethics & Compliance training can work as an "ethical vaccination", as the positive attitude will not be activated now, but stays as "antibodies" inside the person and help to make it immune to the regarding temptations. To ensure an effective protection, such vaccinations must be repeated from time to time.

It must be clear, thanks to these measures, the risk of non-adequate behavior gets reduced, but not to zero. Due to associate professor Morela Hernandez, individuals are not possible to concentrate on short and long-value on the same time, as our brains are not hardwired for such a possibility.[18] As conclusions, it is most relevant that management's tone-from-the-top, in the company or racing-team, ensures that the individuals focus on the championship and not the single lap or race.

---

[18] Hernandez, Morela (2018): "The Impossibility of Focusing on Two Things at Once"

Patrick Henz

8 *"FACTORIES ARE MADE OF PEOPLE, MACHINES AND BRICKS. FERRARI IS MADE MOSTLY OF PEOPLE."*

Born 1898, Enzo Ferrari was clearly a leader of the past century. But nevertheless, his life stays relevant, as big parts of his business philosophy are shared by today's leaders like Steve Jobs, Bill Gates or Richard Branson. It is interesting here is that these people not only live and lived nearly half a century later than Enzo but furthermore have and had been active in completely different cultural regions and types of business.[19]

Integrity based leadership is not always comfortable for the employees (as it can be quite direct with clearly defined rules & responsibilities), but it is an important success-factor for the company. Due to the brand evaluation consultancy "Brand Finance", Ferrari is the world's most powerful brand today. With an overall ranking of AAA+, it received top scores in the

---

[19] Henz, Patrick (2019): "Business Philosophy according to Enzo Ferrari"

categories desirability, loyalty and consumer sentiment to visual identify, online presence and employee satisfaction; just as Enzo described it as *"elite works."* Being leader in these categories allow the company to sell their cars with attractive margins and use the prancing horse further for other merchandising such as clothes, watches and even strollers. As Brand Finance CEO David Haigh stated: *"The prancing horse on a yellow badge is instantly recognizable the world over, even where paved roads have yet to reach. In its home country and among its many admirers worldwide Ferrari inspires more than just brand loyalty, more of a cultish, even quasi-religious devotion, its brand power is indisputable."*[20]

The Ferrari Corporation is not the exception, but the rule that integrity leads to profitable and sustainable business. According to research by Simon Webley and Elise More, companies with an explicit commitment to conduct business ethically presented from 1997 to 2001 a 18% higher profit/turnover ratios than the ones without such a commitment.[21]

In 2019, Ferrari achieved the second position at Forbes' "The World's Best Regarded Companies." This index includes the opinions of 15,000 surveyed individuals from over 50 countries about trustworthiness, social conduct, performance of the company's product or services, and the employer as employer.[22]

Due to another study from 2018, Ferrari achieves an average profit of 69,000 USD/car.[23] This makes it clear that clients not only pay for the physical product, but also the image, including the myth. Based on history and experience, the consumer trusts the product to deliver similar or better performance now and in the future than in the perceived past. Paying for the non-physical part of the product is rational and even compatible with the homo-economicus. As conclusion, if clients pay a premium for the product (physical good plus the emotional charged image), the company

---

[20] Brand Finance (2020): "Ferrari – The World's Most Powerful Brand"

[21] Webley, Simon / More, Elise (2003): "Does Business Ethics Pay?"

[22] Murphy, Andrea (2019): "The World's Best Regarded Companies"

[23] WirtschaftsWoche (2018): "Ferrari macht 69.000 Euro Gewinn pro Auto"

cannot rely only on its physical production-lines, but must focus on its employees' knowledge, integrity and creativity. Enzo perfectly understood this: *"Factories are made of people, machines and bricks. Ferrari is made mostly of people."*

With this understanding he anticipated Industry 4.0. Even if this is no revolution, it is nevertheless an important step inside the continuous industrial evolution. In contrast to earlier, now computer & machines are designed to adapt to the human employee and not the other way around. Of course, jobs get automated, but the remaining employees get fostered, as human characteristics such as curiosity, passion, integrity creativity and critical thinking become imperative for the sustainable success of the corporation.

Furthermore, actual developments such as 3D-printing, the cloud and crowd-sourcing decrease still existing economics of scale. Depending the industry and solution, it is not mandatory anymore to invest in production-lines and machinery. New business models are on the market, so that companies do not directly have to invest in fixed inventory but shift this investment to the supplier. As result, the company only pays for the produced goods. In future, extended production lines may get obsolete, as thanks to 3D-printing even small companies can craft required parts out of different materials, including steel and titanium. Indeed, bricks and machines lose their importance in comparison to the human factor.

Due to a lack of innovation, most disruption comes from industry outsiders and startup-companies. As around 90% of startups fail, most bigger companies are quite relaxed and prefer to study the outcome of these new organizations. When it is predictable that their new products and solutions may succeed on the market, they start to act. To achieve this, there are different strategies:
- Develop me-too products with existing internal resources
- Develop me-too products with external resources
- Develop me-too products with acquiring internal resources from the startup
  - Acquire the startup
  - Try to push with aggressive marketing the startup out of the market

In their early years, startups are financially vulnerable, as they had to invest into the technical development and infrastructure. Salaries are still low and may include stocks. Furthermore, work-life-balance is up to non-existence, as individuals often work unpaid overtime, including week-ends.

To lure these talents away, big companies can offer big possibilities, such as attractive salaries and big budgets to develop their ideas.

Because of the Ferrari myth, Formula 1 drivers normally have two big goals: 1) winning the championship and 2) winning the championship with Ferrari. After Michael Schumacher won 1994 and '95 the championship, he decided to leave his comfort zone and change for the next season to the Ferrari team, even if they had not been competitive at that time. *"I will do everything I can to bring the Number One to Ferrari. The whole team and all the fans deserve it."* He gave up his established position at Benetton, with an exceptionally good forecast of winning the championship again, but to start a long term adventure with Ferrari, being aware that the first years he might not be able again to win the season, but step-by-step had to develop the team together with other key-employees. *"When you start out in a team, you*

have to get the teamwork going and then you get something back." Result: Five championships from 2000 to 2004. Of course, Ferrari offered him a high salary, but the main reason for Michael's choice to change the employer was that he wanted to be part of the myth. As Jean Alesi said before: *"That was my dream, to drive for Ferrari"* and Kimi Räikkönen later: *"If I could have won five or six titles with another team, I would still take this only one with Ferrari".* Besides the emotional part, Schumacher understood Ferrari's strategy to become champion, including various internal changes organized by the still new CEO of the Scuderia Ferrari, Jean Todt (coming in 1993 from Peugeot Talbot Sport), and the joining of other key-players like the technical director Ross Brawn (also from the Benetton team).

This example shows that employees not just work for the money. A phenomenon that Herzberg's "Two-Factor-Theory" wants to explain. According to the scientist, there are two independent factors, one can explain the motivation of the employee and the other one the job dissatisfaction. As result, Herzberg argued that in the working environment exist "motivators" and "hygiene factors".[24] As each human being is different, there exist distinctive factors which can motivate, as for example challenging projects, recognition, responsibility, an office with a view, or maybe just an additional flower. In contrast to this, the hygiene factors bring not additional motivations, but cause demotivation if they are not given, for example regular unpaid overtime or missing job-safety. The salary is a special factor. It can be seen has hygiene, but also as an indirect motivation factor, as money gives the employee the opportunity to acquire their personal motivation factors.

---

[24] Herzberg, Frederick / Mausner, Bernard / Snyderman, Barbara (1959): „The Motivation to Work"

This theory has a high relevance for the manager, as he or she should be aware what are the employees' motivators, the reason they are inside the company and what are their personal goals. If possible, a manager should have at least semi-annual one-on-one interviews with the employees to understand their needs and ideas. For Enzo, he answered this question alone: *"Racing amuses me."*

Entrepreneurs start their own companies not only to ensure income but also based on a vision. They perceive the opportunity to change the market, or even the world as their new products and solutions offer a unique benefit. As conclusion, they are not in for quick win but plan long-term with a focus on sustainability to maximize the long-term value. To ensure a positive and efficient corporate culture, long-established companies shall look back and learn from their founders, even if they lived a century ago.

Enzo Ferrari analyzed his business success: *"Factories are made of people, machines and bricks. Ferrari is made mostly of people."* A modern approach, especially in times of Industry 4.0. Business consultant and MIT-professor MIT professor W. Edwards Deming confirmed the employee's key-position with the four pillars of his "System of Profound Knowledge":

- Appreciation for a system
- Knowledge about variation
- Theory of Knowledge
- Psychology[25]

This approach is based on his diverse background as engineer, statistician and management consultant. Important is that all four points interact with each other and so the sorted mathematical world of the system stands in direct contact with the philosophical knowledge ("Epistemology") and human psychology.

The foundation is the system, planned by Deming from the supplier via the production assembly up to the consumer. Thanks to the detailed knowledge about systems and all factors that can influence them, we are able to plan and manage it as efficiently as possible. Including information and

---

[25] Deming, William Edwards (1993): "The New Economics for Industry, Governance, Education"

experience, changes inside the process are not randomized, but are based on a theory (where the change should take place, what it would provoke and how it would affect the total efficiency) and get measured. To do so, it is not only necessary to predict the output of the potential change, but have a complete overview, which changes are available to execute.

The first two pillars are mathematically based and could be interpreted as a dehumanization of the working environment. To avoid such effect, Deming added philosophy and psychology as third and fourth pillars. This not only underlines the essential importance of the human factor, but also, he defined that all the four pillars had the same importance and due to this, only their holistic connection ensures sustainable success. *"They interact with each other. A change in on part cause changes in other parts."*[26][27]

We can assume that Enzo Ferrari had neither a book of internal norms & regulations, nor a written code of conduct with defined corporate values, as he founded Ferrari S.p.A. in 1947. As there were only a handful of employees, such documents were not been necessary. Everyone had direct contact with *"il Commendatore"* and understood what he expected from the employees. With business success came rising workload and number of employees. Enzo had not the time anymore to explain each employee what to do, so it became necessary to write work-manuals. Strict Italian labor-laws and unions furthermore required to define workers rights and requirements, tax laws require to establish efficient accounting, and so on. To ensure that everybody knows and follow's Enzo's vision, it was imperative to define his values as corporate values. Still today they are defined on the company's website:

- Individual & Team
- Emotion & Integrity
- Tradition & Innovation
- Passion & Excellence[28]

The company's Code of Conduct defines the various norms and expected

---

[26] Canard, Frédéric (2011): "W.E. Deming, Pragmatism and sustainability"

[27] Henz, Patrick (2019): "Tomorrow's Business Ethics – Philip K. Dick vs. W. Edwards Deming"

[28] Ferrari S.p.A. (2020): "Values"

behavior. All other internal regulations base on the CoC. The various documents are based on the founder and represent his values, attitudes, experience and knowledge. Employees should not receive these documents and regulations only as a bureaucratic system, for this it is imperative to emotionalize them. For Ferrari, corporate values manifest in the prancing horse. An important picture not only for clients, but also for employees, providers and other partners.

Aligned with its founder's vision, Ferrari S.p.A. understands that high tech performance products can only be ensured by empowered and appreciated employees.[29] The result of this idea was launched in 1997: "Formula Uomo" (Italian for "Formula Human"). Beyond implementing a pure EHS-program, the company focuses on the humanizing of workplace, combining physical and psychological well-being. The last is a relevant point, also as more governments (for example Mexico) make this a priority. Countries update labor laws to foster psychological well-being inside the companies, including making violations sanction-able.

Thanks to digitization, many monotonous tasks get automated, and employees can focus on human tasks, such as creativity and ingenuity. To foster these skills, the architecture must be human, too. Ferrari reaches this goal by introducing as much nature as possible, for example with integrating natural light, internal garden landscape and natural ventilation.

Ferrari also addresses another relevant pillar of Deming's system: "Theory of Knowledge", the need for continuous learning. Employees receive discounts on school- and university-textbooks. Furthermore, they can learn various foreign languages at lunch-time.

---

[29] OSHA Case Studies: "Wellbeing programme at Ferrari – Formula Uomo"

9 DEMING AND THE PERFECT PIT-STOP

In 1947, W. Edwards Deming met the Japanese culture, as the US Department of Army asked him to plan the later Japanese Census. He always stayed connected with the country, what should be for the mutual benefit, as clearly the Japanese culture also influenced his later theories and publications, including his famous "System of Profound Knowledge".[30] Here he connected the understanding and appreciation of a system together with the philosophical theory of knowledge and psychology. In contrast to the early ages of automation, Deming included the employee not only inside the system, but he also defined him/her as a key part of it. A sign of respect for humanity itself. This philosophy is confirming with the Japanese Shinto-religion, which understands the human as part of nature and environment.[31] Based on Shinto, the Japanese culture developed the idea of "chowa" (Japanese for "a spirit of harmonious partnership"). In a connected world each action leads to a counter-action and, similar to the "butterfly-effect", has numerous consequences.[32] To ensure sustainable and responsible growth, it is imperative to create win-win-situations between the directly involved partners, including to consider the benefit of other potential stakeholders, which do not have a voice or "seat the table".

Despite this connection of philosophies, Deming's ideas work also in Western cultures, including for the most individual employees, like for example race drivers.

In 1935 Tazio Nuvolari won, what later should get named the "impossible victory". With an, at that time, technically inferior Alfa Romeo P3 he made the best race of his career and bet the complete competition on the world's most difficult race-track, the more than 20km long Nürburgring, known as

---

[30] Deming, William Edwards (1993): "The New Economics for Industry, Governance, Education"

[31] Ito, Joi (2018): "Why Westerners fear Robots and the Japanese do not"

[32] Omiya, Hideaki (2018): "Chowa: A Business Philosophy to Bridge a Fractured World"

the "green hell". This is an example that beside strong teams, sometimes one single person can make a difference. Still today, to win the championship it is not enough to have the best machine, you also need the best driver, who is able to unleash the full potential of the car.

A typical task for a manager of a racing team is to have on the one hand a perfect functional team, and on the other hand to integrate the most talented drivers, who in many cases, are not born team-players.

On the race-track the drivers are connected to their team and depend on its advice to decide when to attack, but also when to save fuel or protect the tires. Nevertheless, the driver stays dominant, as the information gets considered, but the decision is made on the individual's experience and judgement of the situation. Formula One driver Kimi Räikkönen became famous in 2012 for his answer to his Lotus Formula One box crew, as he received too many messages while driving: *"Leave me alone, I know what I'm doing."*

But the situation changes for the mandatory pit-stops, and not only for the stop itself, already for the planning. The team includes experts using sophisticated algorithms to calculate the car's actual performance, fuel reserves, tire degradation and many other factors. Not only for the own car, in addition the main competitors get observed to predict their strategies, including timing and number of pit-stops. This is to adapt the own strategy to the competitors and other external factors, like starting rainfalls or safety car-phases due to an accident.

Vision Formula 1, with friendly permission from Mark Andar.

With turning into the pit-lane, the individual star driver temporally loses the outstanding position and becomes an ordinary team-member. It is his or her task to steer the car at the required speed (maximum 80 km/h) exactly to the spot where the mechanics are already waiting. Formula One champion Juan Manuel Fangio went one step further: *"The driver of a racing car is a component."* Even if discussable for the whole race, for the process of the pit-stop, it brings the situation to the point.

There are three mechanics at each wheel, one to open and close the locks of the rims, one to take off the used tire and one to put on the new one. In addition to this, there is one mechanic at the back of the car to lift it up (due to Formula 1 regulations are no powered units allowed here) and two on the side of the car to safe-guard the process.

The team, including the drivers, practice this process repeatedly, so that each little step works in perfection and the different individuals work as one. The aim is to act as precisely as possible, so that each time the process can get executed exactly as practiced, because every small variation would lead to a longer standing time for car and driver. These numerous repeats in training are required so that the team-members know "blindly" each handle. The process gets as little cognitive as possible. Not only that there is no time for thinking, furthermore everyone in the race is full of adrenaline. This is required for humans to go to the limit inside the competition but has the downside that the high level of stress may block the individual's capability for logical thinking. Rigorous training-units simulate all predictable scenarios. Team members learn the "scripts" for each different situation, extended decision-making processes get avoided.

The results of the efforts are 2.09 seconds during pit-stops. As it would be impossible for a human to control the fast-paced process, an electronic device observes the different steps. When it concludes that they had been all executed correctly, it gives the driver the sign to accelerate, leave the box and return on the race-track.

Most of the TV-cameras are on the two drivers, as they have an outstanding position inside the team. This is justified, as their individual talent is required, and they take on the highest risks for the project. Nevertheless, more is required to win a championship, a holistic approach as it was defined by Deming in his "System of Profound Knowledge".[33]

---

[33] Deming, William Edwards (1993): "The New Economics for Industry, Governance, Education"

10 THE RACE TWIN

Digital Twins are nearly every to find, even in places least expected. One of them is Formula One. To reduce costs, regulations strictly limit physical testing between the races, even on private race-tracks. As in the sports even details can decide between winning and losing, teams constantly analyze guidelines to understand where the thin red lines are. As result, if physical testing is not possible, virtual one must do the job.

All major teams invested into simulation centers, where replicas are mounted on moving ground and connected to high tech computers. This concept is like a typical Digital Twin, as used in different industries. There is a twist, these twins are not all virtual but include a physical part. Nevertheless, creating such a simulator requires the same two steps:

The Digital & Physical Model, an original creation of the model, which should understand, predict and / or optimize (based on General Electric's definition of a Digital Twin) a real or fictive object or process. This step includes a first data model, a set of analytics or algorithms, and knowledge. To reach this, a mixed team of engineers and IT-experts must work jointly to create a simulator, which not only virtually reacts like the original, but also physically handles the same. Simulator manufacturer fFpro uses Lidar laser measurement technology to scan the environment and realistically simulate it. As race teams can use more time to scan their own private race-tracks, like Ferrari's Fiorano, they can be better simulated with more details than the other race-tracks.[34] Due to this, even in the virtual world, such own tracks keep their importance.

Digital Shadowing connects the Digital Twin with the physical model. A modern F1 car can have between 150 & 300 sensors and send this information to the team. In contrast to a classic Digital Twin, the Formula One simulator can only receive data on limited occasions when the physical

---

[34] Rfpro.com (fetched 4.2.2018): "LiDAR Survey"

car is allowed to be used. This can be in training, but also directly in the race itself. The more information, the simulator receives, the more it can analyze the car's performance, but also the better the model can be calibrated and update the model to make it as realistic as possible.

The simulator helps the team to understand their car inside limited time. This tests different updates and setups to create an advantage for the race weekend. To reach this goal, it is required that also the so called "simulation driver" is experienced with real Formula 1 cars. For example, in 2018 the Ferrari team had Sebastian Vettel and Kimi Räikkönen as their driver combination for the championships, and Antonio Giovinazzi as simulation driver. To qualify for this position, Giovinazzi not only participated successfully in Ferrari's Driver Academy, but also participated in two races of the 2017 season for the Sauber Ferrari-team.[35] Being the third driver not only includes being behind the monitor, but few times also testing the physical car. With this, the driver can understand how close original and twin really are. If not restricted by Formula 1 guidelines, to optimize the benefit of the twin, the simulation driver could support over the race-weekend the team while using similar setups on the simulated track. To enhance the simulation ("Augmented Virtualilty" as opposite of "Augmented Reality"), the program not only uses real-time information from the race-car but include also original weather information.

---

[35] Anderson, Ben (2018): "Ferrari F1 reserve Giovinazzi keen to prove he's not just sim driver"

With the boundaries between the virtual and physical world vanishing, in 2019 Giovinazzi switches sides and participated in the Formula One-championship for the Alfa Romeo-team, a long-side his further team colleague Kimi Räikkönen. His seat at the simulator had been taken by four drivers: Pascal Wehrlein (Sauber F1 / Formula E / DTM), Brendon Hartley (F1 Scuderia Toro Rosso / Le Mans), Antonio Fuoco (Formula 1) and Davide Rigon (FIA WEC / simulation driver since 2014).[36] A diverse group to infuse a maximum of various experiences into the development of the team, including its simulator.

---

[36] Ferrari.com (fetched 4.2.2019): "Four drivers for Scuderia Ferrari simulator"

11 THE UNDERCUT

In motor-sports, especially Formula One, the "undercut" is a strategy to gain an advantage based on an earlier pit-stop. For example, in the case that driver A leads driver B. The second may be faster, but this is not enough for a successful overtaking of A. Taking different sources of information into account, like the car's performance, the competitors' behaviors, weather-forecast, type of tires, etc., the team elaborates the ideal race strategy.

US president Dwight D. Eisenhower once stated: *"Planning is everything. The plan is nothing."* Of course, this is also true for race-strategies. As men and machines are constantly at the limit, the overall-situation is always changing. Even small technical issues or driving errors can lead to the loss of positions. In addition, safety-car or the track or unpredictable changes of weather require an updated strategy. To reach the best strategy, the teams include intelligent algorithms. Artificial Intelligence can only be as good as the data-input. Faster connections, like 5G, support the usage of more sophisticated sensors, as the net supports the transportation of bigger information-packages. Humans and AI elaborate different scenarios and calculate their likelihoods. Thanks to human experience and computers, the strategies and calculated chances are not fixed, but continuously adapt to the actual situation, including information coming from the sensors (like rain on parts of the race-track).

Driver B being stuck behind A is such a scenario, which can lead to a change of strategy. Better information and better algorithms may lead to better insights and higher quality decisions. Driver B's team may calculate an opportunity to win the race if they use a different race-strategy than all its competitors. The last may not even comprehend this, as they do not have access to the same information and/or could interpret it accordingly. The processing of information is a task for the Human-AI Team. Both, human and machine work similarly as they try to relate the received data to existing information, to identify known patterns. In general, the AI is superior in the identification of patterns, the human can better process the data into unique and creative solutions. For the last, the AI may assist the decision-making with presenting standard strategies and probabilities. The human must critically analyze these suggestions to decide whether to take one of them or do something different. Diversity and inclusion support the ability of a team to interpret data and identify the patterns. This includes diversity in the work-groups, which are responsible for the decision-making, but also in the teams which are responsible for designing the AI.

Another relevant factor are the different levels of risk-appetite. The leading driver (not only in the race itself, but the actual championship) typically has a lower risk-appetite. The chaser must find possibilities how he/she could go faster. In the latter phases of the championship, this will include accepting a higher risk-appetite, including executing riskier race-strategies or execute a more optimistic overtake. A higher risk-appetite may also trigger the undercut, as it is a decision different to most other teams. The team brings the driver earlier inside the box with the hope that he/she can use the fresh tires (or slightly changed setup) and go significantly faster the next laps. With this, after the competitor's stop, the former leading driver A returns to the track behind B.

In the world of business, the undercut can be related to disruption. Based on information and its interpretation, companies may conclude that the actual setup is not comparative anymore, but there is the possibility to change strategy and offer something different, relevant for the potential target-group. This disruption can be the product/solution itself, or also inside the production-process, including the usage of different providers.

12 FROM GENTLEMEN DRIVERS TO BETA-TESTERS

It is fascinating to study the past to understand that numerous of today's ideas and processes already existed a long time ago. This also includes business strategies and leaders. *"It is said that whoever does not know history is damned to repeat it. But whoever wants to repeat it is damned to know it."* (Frank Wisniewski) Especially the rich biography of a figure like Enzo Ferrari has many precious lessons for us.

Still part of Alfa Romeo, the Scuderia Ferrari grew up to more than 50 drivers, and with this became the racing department with the most numerous drivers ever. This could be reached as Enzo Ferrari organized them similar to sales executives, meaning they did not gain a fixed salary, but got paid according to their success. Furthermore, a part of them had been so-called "Gentlemen Drivers", wealthy men of the upper classes, which not only had been drivers, but also bought the race cars themselves. Independent from this, their level of talent varied. Some of them could even compete with the hired professional drivers, one of these examples had been Clemente Biondetti. Originally born 1898 into a working-class family, based on his talent he achieved a seat at the Maserati factory team, before he switched to Alfa Romeo. His early success enabled him to invest into race cars, so that he won the Mille Miglia 1938 with a private Alfa Romeo 8C 2900B Spider MM Touring and 1947 with an Alfa Romeo 8C 2900B Berlinetta Touring.

In 1948, the Scuderia Ferrari enrolled two 166 Allemano Mille Miglia. The stronger "SC" was driven by the legendary Tazio Nuvolari, the "S" by the gentlemen driver Clemente Biondetti. Due to technical problems, Nuvolari could not finish the race, what opened the way for Biondetti's third triumph at this traditional event. Due to respect for Nuvolari, Biondetti started this speech at the latter awards dinner with the words *"excuse me for having won."*

Enzo Ferrari once justified motor sports: *"What has instructed all of the world's builders of safe, efficient cars? Auto racing. Any theory, any laboratory experiment needs practical support, and only the race can offer it because during the race the driver submits the car and its parts to intense, unpredictable, unthinkable testing."* For him, the gentlemen drivers had been important for two reasons, they helped to finance the professional racing team, but also they volunteered to test his products. Not only in average use, but right at the limit. This showed already in beginning of his managing career his practical and non-romantic approach. At the same time, we still find this practice today, but in a completely different industry.

Software companies hand-out so-called beta-versions to the most technically involved clients, which volunteer and register for this perceived privilege. In contrast to the gentlemen drivers, these users do not risk their lives, but at least the functionality of their private computer system, as such early software versions still include bugs and other incompatibilities. Due to their knowledge, the beta-testers can give precious feedback to the manufacturer and support the internal development-team to create the final product.

Clemente survived his racing career, and with four victories became the uncrowned "King of the Mille Miglia", including a monument at the Raticosa Pass.

Patrick Henz

13 *"I AM IN LOVE WITH MY CAR."*

In the 2018 Queen biopic "Bohemian Rhapsody",[37] drummer Roger Taylor's song "I am in love with my car"[38] (b-side on "Bohemian Rhapsody[39]) was used as a running gag. On the first view, a catchy song about a man's relation with his car. Later, Roger Taylor mentioned that it was less autobiographic (even if he was a real petrol-head), but a general homage to "boy racers", inspired by the group's roadie.[40]

Interesting fun fact, the song included the engine sound of Taylor's actual car from 1975, an Alfa Romeo Spider. Later he bought various Ferrari, including a 308 GTB.[41]

"The machine of a dream. Such a clean machine."

"My cars have to be beautiful", Enzo Ferrari added to his famous quote that his cars had not only to be beautiful, but also to be fast and reliable. People like to simplify problems. As speed and reliability are not verifiable on a first view, we take our experiences from the past and combine what looks fast with what looks reliable. The result is an idea of beauty, which implies success.

By doing so, we often suffer by a halo-effect. If there is one positive piece of information, in this case the beauty of the car, we assume other positive characteristics like speed and reliability. The view on beauty is shaped by evolution, as survival depended that what is beneficial must be perceived as attractive. Thinking of cars, our view on beauty includes subconsciously

---

[37] Singer, Bryan (2018): "Bohemian Rhapsody"

[38] Taylor, Roger (1975): "I am in Love with my Car."

[39] Mercury, Freddie (1975): "Bohemian Rhapsody"

[40] Songfacts (fetched 2020): "I'm in Love with my Car"

[41] S., Josh (fetched 2020): "I'm in Love with my Car: Roger Taylor and his Cars"

also our technical knowledge. As Kimi Räikkönen stated during the presentation of the 2015 Ferrari Formula One car, the SF15-T: *"It looks nice, and when it looks good it should be a pretty good car."*

Besides temporary fashions, it explains why car designs changed over the time ("form follows function") and why we see today other designs as beautiful than people in the past did. Paul Frère was not only race driver, but also knowledgeable about modern aerodynamics. For this, he did not perceive the 1957 Ferrari 250 Testa Rossa as a beautiful car (as we do in general today), but for his aesthetic sense, it was disturbing that the windshield was designed so steep, disturbing the car's aerodynamics.

"When I'm holding your wheel, all I hear is your gear."

Formula One champion Juan Manuel Fangio once said: *"The driver of a racing car is a component. When I first began, I used to grip the steering wheel firmly, and I changed gear so hard that I damaged my hand."*

A successful race car consists of many different parts, but equally important are the driver's skills. Fangio realized that in reality there is no separation between machine and driver, but they must work as one. As there are different cars and setups available, each human is also different. As result, not each driver is fast with the same car, but the setup depends on the personal driving style.

Due to this, the car's setup must be adapted to new driver. Only if the employee feels 100% comfortable with the machine / program, he / she is able to become one with the system. To have a strong department, it is not required to have the best employees but make them work together. If a highly skilled employee is not able to work with the team, changes must occur; related this employee or the team. At the end an employee, who may look as less qualified on the paper, may contribute to a higher team-output as the better qualified individual who does not fit into the group. It is a sensible task for the manager to make a group of employees a strong performance team.

At the end, Fangio's Formula One career with Ferrari only lasted for one season. He was the strongest driver at that time, and won the driver's title with the Scuderia, but nevertheless he and Enzo Ferrari decided to go separated ways the next year, as due to Fangio's character, he not became an integrated part of the team. There had been tensions between the different drivers, and it was only a question of time until these would have let to a bigger problem. As every individual has a different character, each group has also. Due to this, some people are easy to adapt into a group, but nevertheless this does not automatically mean that this works with all groups.

"COMPLIANCE IS A RACE CAR."

"Compliance is a Race Car.", Patrick Henz, 2019, 3. edition, 188 pages

ISBN-10: 1545157634, ISBN-13: 978-1545157633

The idea of this book is to go further than being a manual for Compliance, as it should work on different levels. Newcomers and experts can learn about the different parts of an effective Ethics & Compliance program. The toolbox questions support the reader to understand if the own program is adequate or requires optimization. Furthermore, the book demonstrates that all parts of the program interact with each other, and the whole is more than the pure addition of the single items.

The book invites the reader to a time travel, as it goes to the past to analyze what Compliance can learn from the structures of a traditional Mafia organization (always keeping in mind that Compliance and Mafia stand on opposite sides). Then it brings us back to the creation of a successful race car, to blast off and investigate the near future to present the new challenges based on robotics and Artificial Intelligence.

The different trips not only underline that "travelling educates" and due to this, Compliance is not a function to stay behind a desk, but furthermore Ethics & Compliance is a task, which can be interpreted based on the own character and offers the required space and flexibility to climb up Maslow's Pyramids.

BUSINESS PHILOSOPHY ACCORDING TO ENZO FERRARI

"An inspiration for managers, leaders and everybody who is interested in Enzo Ferrari's life."

Born 1898 in the Northern-Italian city of Modena, Enzo Ferrari lived his dream and founded the world's most famous sports car manufacturer. This book analyzes how he achieved his goals by what are considered to be modern concepts. Or were leadership theories, emotional intelligence, business ethics, client orientation and sustainability already guiding principles of business in the beginning of the last century.

In his own words, and drawing several parallels to Italian history, he thought he was living in the wrong time. But taking off Il Commendatore's sunglasses, this book presents him as a surprisingly modern leader, who, conscious or not, acted conform the latest business and leadership models, confirmed by key decisions of his company, including the racing-team.

Therefore, the book not only uses racing decisions and car development as examples, including many photos, but sets them in relation to his personal business philosophy.

7. edition, 370 pages, ISBN-10: 1548099074, ISBN-13: 978-1548099077

PEPE, THE RED RACE CAR

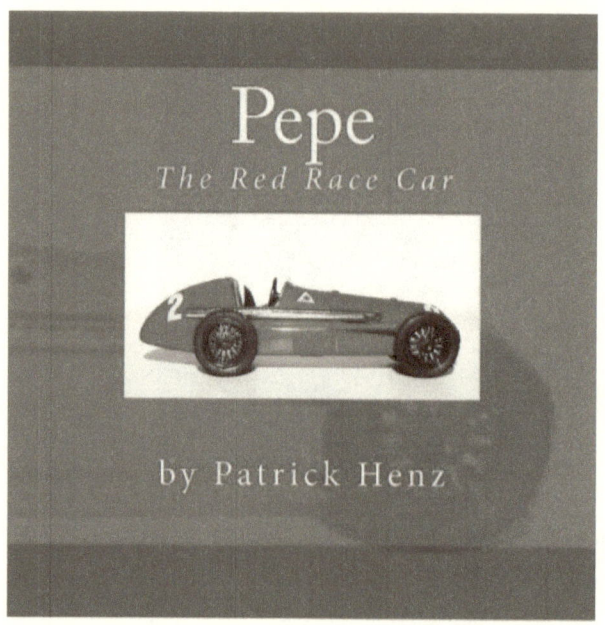

"Pepe, the Red Race Car", Patrick Henz, 2014, 1. edition, 30 pages

ISBN-10: 1503358739, **ISBN-13:** 978-1503358737

Pepe was the fastest race car in the early 1950's and on the best way to win the World Championship. But then his opponent John started to use unfair measures and the deserved success seemed to be out of reach.

Pepe decided not to give up and to fight for his dream and against the corruption! A fast and entertaining book for children of 6 years and older. As ethical or corrupt behavior is learnt already in young years, the story is a good base to discuss this topic with parents or teachers.

ABOUT THE AUTHOR

Patrick Henz started his career in Corporate Information and Compliance at the end of 2007, when he was responsible for the implementation of an Anti-Corruption program in Mexico and several Central American and Caribbean countries. Together with these tasks, he gained valuable insights into global Compliance programs, with a focus on Latin America. Since 2009 in his role as Compliance Officer he is responsible for an effective Compliance program; based on identification, protection, detection, response & recovery and combined with integrity, respect, passion & sustainability. With these means, he defines Compliance as pro-active function, being perceived as guardian, expert and facilitator. The focus is on information to ensure adequate behavior, not only of the human employee, but Artificial Intelligence included.

This includes the regular planning and execution of Compliance Risk Assessments and further global reviews. According an effective sustainability strategy, where Compliance plays a key role, he actively promotes this idea at university workshops and conferences (including the ACI Compliance Boot-Camp 2013, '15 and '17 in Houston). In so doing he became two times President of Honor of Marcus Evans' Latin-American Corporate Compliance Conference 2011 and '12 in Mexico City, panelist at The Economist's Mexico Summit 2015 and co-founder of the Ethics & Compliance Forum Mexico, including editor and co-author of the Ethics & Compliance Manual, published in April 2014.

Since 2013 he lives and works in Atlanta, USA.

www.ingramcontent.com/pod-product-compliance
Lightning Source LLC
Chambersburg PA
CBHW020608220526
45463CB00006B/2504